RAW FOOD FEAST

vibrant health through living foods

raw | vegan | oil-free

MIRJAM HENZEN

Praise for RAW FOOD FEAST

"As a plant-based chef with my greatest passion being raw cuisine, Mirjam's book, Raw Food Feast is incredibly appealing to me, with a lovely range of globally inspired recipes that are also thoughtfully curated to provide optimum health and nutrition. For anyone wishing to enjoy food while also doing wonderful work for their longevity, wellness, and the planet, I highly recommend it!"

- Matthew Kenney, chef

"I own a phenomenal number of books on raw food. You'd be shocked. Now, I am thrilled to add Raw Food Feast to my collection. Mirjam has gone completely over the top with her new book. Rich with detail, filled with brilliant food photography, loaded with health and nutrition information, and so many creative recipes; Mirjam put her full energy into Raw Food Feast and did not hold back at all. This is definitely a book you will want to be able to refer to."

- Dr. Douglas N. Graham, author of The 80/10/10 Diet

"Mirjam Henzen has created a beautiful masterpiece for anyone interested in vibrant, living cuisine. Her strong nutrition background translates over into Raw Food Feast and her recipes. I know the importance of having access to the nutritional information behind a raw food diet so that you can do it properly, and Mirjam has done an excellent job of explaining this in Raw Food Feast. All the tips she provides at the beginning of the book are invaluable and will have you executing her recipes with ease. The recipes are simple without compromising flavor; even if you have never made raw foods before you will have no problem making these! I also love her spin on the recipe and chapter names; they are so creative and get you excited to dive into the recipes. Congratulations on this beautiful book Mirjam!
Anyone who is interested in adopting more living foods into their life needs this book; you will love her mouth-watering recipes."

- Crystal Bonnet, creator of Crystal Dawn Culinary and author of The Art of Raw Desserts

Praise for RAW FOOD FEAST

"I have spent many years of my life teaching the importance of a raw food diet to health, and Raw Food Feast is a must-have book for finding fun, healthy, exciting raw food recipes to enjoy. There are so many great recipes in this book, for everyone from a seasoned raw food enthusiast to a beginner who is just starting on their journey! I always tell people to make health a passion and keep it fun and exciting, and these recipes are a great example of how much fun you can have on a raw food lifestyle! Be love and enjoy the journey!"

- Dr. Robert Morse, N.D., D.Sc., M.H.

"As a raw vegan since 1994, I look only for the best raw food resources. I love Mirjam Henzen's beautifully designed raw food health and recipe book Raw Food Feast. Mirjam knows what our bodies need to thrive, which is clearly seen in this collection of colorful, delicious recipes that will make the raw vegan lifestyle easy and successful for everyone."

- Karen Ranzi, M.A., award-winning author of Creating Healthy Children: Through Attachment Parenting and Raw Foods

Hey health lover,

Welcome to the wonderful world of living foods! I am incredibly thankful you are holding this funky recipe collection of raw plant food deliciousness in your hands. I cannot wait for you to dive in and to 'ooh!' and 'aah!' your way through every bite you are about to taste.

I have a few big loves in life. Obviously, raw food is one of them. But I also love to listen to some fine tunes. The thing is, I am not just a full-time foodie, but melodies and lyrics make my heart beat faster too. Soul, funk, jazz, you name it, I like it all. In Raw Food Feast, I have brought those two worlds together. You can even hop on Spotify to groove along with the one and only Raw Food Feast Playlist while creating these scrumptious recipes! Check the colophon on page 165 for the link/code to dance your way into the kitchen.

For the best results, it is recommended to start by reading the two chapters, on pages 8 and 15, before you get your party started. 'Unlock the path to vibrant health' is all about the benefits of healthy living, ways to speed up the dehydration process, and saving money, in the meantime. Next, I will guide you on using the recipes with helpful tips to make your raw food feast a grand success.

And in closing, maybe just maybe, you have wondered: how to pronounce her name? No worries, I get it. It always gets butchered because most other languages, unlike Dutch, have no such thing as a 'J' after an 'R'.
My name is pronounced as Miriam. (Thanks, mom and dad ;-))

Enjoy your raw food feast!

Love and vibrant health,
Mirjam

Contents

SMASHING SOUPS

souper power that makes you wanna dance

BANGER SALADS

saladbrate good times!

FUNKY BITES

bites to the beat of your own drum

Contents

Unlock the path to vibrant health

It is easier than it ever has been to immerse yourself with information about healthy living. The problem with this wealth of data is the many different views and opinions on this topic. There is much to say about healthy living. This important topic deserves a book on its own, but I will share my two cents to give you an idea of why I believe we unlock the path to vibrant health through living foods.

The law of nature

If we want to discover what health truly is, we should check what nature shows us. In the animal-kingdom animals eat everything in its natural state, for example. They know what foods to eat and what things to leave untouched. Instinctively they know that not everything found in nature is meant for their species. When they feel sick, they rest and fast until they are better again.

I believe that we, humans, also instinctively know what our needs are, but that our ability is dimmed because we have strayed away from the law of nature that empowers our receptors or antennas, as it were.

Over time we have created many tools and processes that have enabled us to get creative with foods like fruit, greens, vegetables, nuts, seeds, and seaweeds. The downside is that we have also made inedible things edible. Plus, numerous people eat animals and their products on a large scale. This way of eating is causing all sorts of troublesome symptoms like digestive issues, burned-out adrenal glands, and kidneys that do not filter well, to name a few. All of which can result in poor health. We have strayed far from the law of nature and the way we should consume foods in general.

The protein myth

Let me explain where I come from when I say that we have strayed far from our natural diet and why I believe a high raw fruit and plant food lifestyle is the best and only wise way of living.

Our beautiful foods, such as ripe water-rich fruit and fresh leafy greens, are loaded with vitamins, minerals, amino acids, fiber, and enzymes. We all know we need plenty of vitamins and minerals to be healthy. Unfortunately, there is also misinformation out in the world that tells us we need lots of protein every day. It is not the case. What we need are amino acids, the building blocks of protein. Now you might think, is that not the same? It is not. Our body is not capable of using proteins right away.

Plus, an overload of proteins is harming our health. When we consume lots of protein, especially those found in animal products, our body needs to work hard to break down all these proteins into amino acids. Next, these amino acids are turned into proteins the body can use.

This process puts a massive strain on our digestive system. Also, proteins are harsh on the kidneys, are mucus-forming, and leave behind acid ash. The ash is the residue left in the body from the food or product we consume, meaning it has an acidic effect on the cells of your beautiful body.

Alkalinity for the win

Your body exists out of two fluids (the lymphatic and blood system) and a whole bunch of cells. Those cells make up your digestive system, kidneys, adrenal glands, and so on. Your lymph fluid flushes waste and toxins through eliminative organs, such as the kidneys, colon, and skin. Poor diet choices, a weak gut microbiome, and all sorts of toxic influences cause the lymphatic system to become congested and stagnant. The result is that mucus and acids will be formed, and so-called diseases are born.

The overall state of your body should be alkaline. There is one place in the body that should be acidic: the stomach. Unfortunately, many people deal with low stomach acid, which means it is leaning toward the alkaline side. Other body parts, which naturally should be in an alkaline state, are experiencing various levels of acidity, which causes all sorts of trouble that the medical world labels as a disease. These imbalances are mostly caused by diet. However, other factors also play a role, such as skin care products.

Just as most of your body needs to be alkaline for overall health, it is equally important to have normal levels of hydrochloric acid in the stomach. Stomach acid enables several crucial processes in the body. The absorption of most minerals is one of them. Many people are dealing with parasites and fungi. In a healthy body, parasites and fungi will not survive, as a healthy level of stomach acid will deal with it right away.

Leafy greens are a huge blessing to your health. They are vitally important to obtain and maintain normal levels of stomach acid. Leafy greens also increase your fiber and mineral intake.

Symptoms from ailments and diseases are expressions of the body calling for help. Your body is communicating that its environment has become acidic and thus unhealthy. It craves the food it's made for: mostly ripe water-rich fruit and fresh leafy greens. Our bodies need and thrive on raw fruit and plant food because of its alkalinity and perfect ratios of carbs, fat, and protein. Besides, raw fruit and plant foods are also packed with fiber.

More than a broom

Gladly, there's a rising interest in the role of fiber and its great benefits.
Fiber is a crucial factor in vibrant health. Often fiber is just referred to as a broom for the colon. But it is so much more than that. Fiber is fuel to your gut microbiome. It feeds the bacteria in your gut microbiome and creates microbiome diversity.
Your gut plays a vital role in your overall health, as a massive part of your immune system will weaken or strengthen by the condition of your gut microbiome. We need fiber desperately every single day.
Most people lack the daily-needed amount of fiber in their diet, resulting in a weak gut microbiome. One of its results is that the gut cannot fight off the simplest bacteria and/or viruses that can form a threat to health. Raw foods like ripe water-rich fruit, leafy greens, fresh veggies, and crisp sprouts are full of fiber. By consuming predominantly a wide variety of raw fruit and plant food, you feed your gut with the fiber it needs.

Most of the recipes in Raw Food Feast assist in strengthening your gut microbiome due to the ingredients used. For example, psyllium husk is a perfect aid for digestion and is full of fiber. It also works as a natural binder in recipes, making it a win-win situation.

The life force

Besides vitamins, minerals, amino acids, and fiber, raw fruit, and plant foods are full of enzymes. Enzymes are the life force in our food and our bodies. When we heat food at high temperatures, it will destroy the enzymes and partially the nutrients.
However, as with many other things in life, not all enzymes are created equally. There are many different types of enzymes, each of which has its function and task. Furthermore, one enzyme can tolerate more heat than another before it loses its power.

There are various theories In the raw food world about the ideal temperature to prepare food in a dehydrator. Viktoras Kulvinskas, nutritionist and co-founder of the Hippocrates Health Institute, has extensively tested the effect of heat on enzymes and has concluded that certain enzymes can be exposed to temperatures of about 149 °F/65 °C without loosing their power.

Ann Wigmore, who co-founded the Hippocrates Health Institute with Viktoras, has come to similar conclusions. Through all sorts of tests, Ann discovered when the food temperature rose above 118 °F/48 °C for a longer time, this usually destroyed the enzymes. She also noticed that the best technique to keep enzymes intact is to set the dehydrator to a higher food temperature at the beginning of the drying process and then adjust the temperature to a lower setting after a few hours.

However, because most people may not know when to lower the dehydrator and thus leave the dehydrator at a (too) high temperature too long, which could still destroy the enzymes, she suggested setting the dehydrator at 105 °F/41 °C during the entire drying process. In this way, the food temperature never exceeds 118 °F/48 °C.

You can set the dehydrator temporarily at a higher temperature without destroying the enzymes because of the difference between the food and air temperature. The dehydrator distributes heated air over the food during the drying process. The heat causes the food to cool initially through evaporation.

You can compare it to a beautiful summer day. You are outside and warm, and you take a dip in the sea. As soon as you get out of the water, you get cold, despite the heat of the sun. The difference between your body temperature and the outside air causes this effect.

The food and air temperature also differ from one another. By temporarily increasing the temperature, the food dries faster, the dehydration process takes less time, which is more economical, and ensures the preservation of nutrients, enzymes, and taste.

For this reason, I regularly advise you to use a higher temperature for only a few hours when creating a recipe. If, for whatever reason, you do not feel comfortable with this way of drying food, adjust the dehydration temperatures and times according to your liking.

It is clear that enzymes are of utmost importance for vibrant health and that cooking food is one of the factors that can be detrimental to your wellbeing. I do not think that cooked whole plant foods are poisonous or harmful. Having said that, I am convinced that we should consume most of our daily food in its natural raw state to unlock the path to vibrant health. However, there is another critically important factor to consider when cooking food.

To cook or not to cook?

Paul Kouchakoff, a Swiss doctor, led a profound study on the direct effect of cooking food on the immune system. He discovered that white blood cells mobilize and increase as an immune response when we digest cooked food. Raw fruit and plant foods fail to cause this immune response, called digestive leukocytosis, and will prevent cooked foods from creating such a response when eaten together.

By digesting cooked foods as the majority per meal, your body responds to it as a foreign organism. It puts an unnecessary burden on the immune system. If you choose to eat cooked food, it is wise to do so in combination with raw food to prevent this unwanted reaction in the body.

If you want to unlock the path to vibrant health, your diet should consist primarily of ripe water-rich fruits and leafy greens. Fresh veggies, crisp sprouts, salty seaweeds, and healthy fats from avocados, coconuts, seeds, and nuts are perfect add-ons.

Living foods offer the best and easiest solution to strengthen your gut microbiome and support the lymphatic system to detoxify. It is because raw fruit and plant foods contain vitamins, minerals, amino acids, fiber, and enzymes. These elements support the gut and lymphatic system to work as nature intended.

When it comes to raw food, especially ripe water-rich fruit and fresh leafy greens have an incredible effect on your well-being. They help the body eliminate acids, regenerate tissues, and hydrate on a cellular level. Alkalizing fruit and leafy greens move the lymphatic system, break up stagnation, and flush toxins.

An easy way to increase the nutrient intake for your cells and your gut microbiome is by adding sprouts to your smoothies and salads, for example. These little powerhouses are full of nutrients and fiber.

Today is the best day to start adding more raw ripe water-rich fruit and fresh leafy greens to your day-to-day to gain and maintain a thriving immune system. Remember, health is just a step away.

The perfect fuel

Refined sugar wreaks havoc on your health. It wrecks your metabolism, ruins your skin, puts a massive strain on your adrenal glands, which causes anxiety and depression in the long run, and your endocrine system (hormones) will be in disarray.

Ripe water-rich fruit and fresh leafy greens should be your number one food choice. You need sugar in abundance. Your body functions mainly on sugar. Unrefined sugar from ripe fruit and fresh plant food is your natural fuel. It is perfect and beneficial for you and essential for energy production for your cells. Fruit is not just a snack. It can be enjoyed as a proper meal.

The way to go

Not that long ago, high-fat diets made their rise, and swaying thousands upon thousands of people to join this trend to lose weight. It is crazy, but fruit is now labeled as a food that is too high in sugar, and you should be careful not to eat too much of it, plus it will make you fat. Instead, if you want to lose weight, you should eat a ton of fat. It is the world upside down, and we need to set the record straight.

Many people consume products that are high-fat, high-calorie, and nutrient lacking. It is not just people who follow a specific high-fat diet who fall into this category. When you eat quite some processed and animal products, you gain body fat quickly, and acidosis will develop rapidly, causing all sorts of health issues. Even though fats from whole foods, like avocados, coconuts, nuts, and seeds, are the ones we should consume, it does not mean we should bulk on those. A high-fat diet is just not a wise idea.

You might wonder why there are so many people who, initially, see results in weight loss in the ketogenic scene. It's mainly due to giving up all the refined carbs. A high-fat diet is not a long-term sustainable diet. Nature is the best guidance for your nutritional intake. It clearly shows that a high-carb, low-fat diet is the way to go.

A diet high in carbs and low in fat means you enjoy a low-fat intake, not a zero fat intake. Fats from fruits, plants, nuts, and seeds are healthy fats, and you need them. The thing is that in today's society, the proportions are totally out of whack. There is a high focus on protein, the wrong kind of carbs, and in general, people consume a ton of fat, which are often not even the good fats that are beneficial to our health and wellbeing. As said before: if we want to discover what health truly is, we best observe what nature shows us.

When you check the ratios of breastmilk, you'll find that breastmilk is high in sugar (carbs), low in fat, and even lower in protein. Nature is the best guidance for your nutritional intake, meaning a high-carb and low-fat diet.

Symptoms of so-called ailments and diseases are rampant, crippling people's healt around the world and are telling us that we are not lining up with the laws of nature. It shows us that people are overly acidic, thus having strayed away from how God intended it to be.

Isn't it crazy, then, that we change those ratios and call it a healthy diet? We need a diet rich in simple carbs and low in fat. The good news is that we can make thoughtful lifestyle changes every single day. We can gain and maintain vibrant health by embracing an alkaline diet consisting of lots of raw fruit and plant food.

How to use the recipes and helpful tips

Prepping ingredients

Wash all fruits, greens, and vegetables before use. Soak them in some soda bicarbonate and water, then give them a good rinse. It helps to remove unwanted chemicals. Remove linseeds from bell peppers, peel carrots with a vegetable peeler, just like cucumber and other ingredients, unless indicated otherwise.

Soaking nuts, seeds, and legumes

Nature is beautiful. It is evident when we look at nuts, seeds, and legumes, for example. They contain a thin layer known as enzyme inhibitors/phytic acid. It protects against insects or a pest and prevents them from (prematurely) germinating. This same clever layer is less pleasant for your body because it inhibits the working of enzymes and the absorption of nutrients, such as zinc, calcium, and iron. It also makes these types of food more difficult to digest. Soaking nuts, seeds, and legumes remove this protective layer. It also increases enzyme activity and makes nutrients easier to absorb and digest. But that is not all because soaked nuts and seeds puree much better in the blender, and you will taste the difference. Dips, dressings, and sauces will be smoother and creamier.

All the recipes indicate how long you should soak the nuts, seeds, or legumes.

I especially like to work with buckwheat and green lentils when it comes to sprouting, besides the more commonly used sprouts, such as alfalfa or pea shoots. Both buckwheat and green lentils are nutritional powerhouses and fun using to create recipes.
Another benefit is that buckwheat is not wheat but a seed and thus gluten-free. Meaning, it does not act like glue as grains and wheat actually do.

Usually, hummus is made with chickpeas. And even though chickpeas can be sprouted and eaten raw, most digestive systems do not respond well to it. Gladly, this is not the case with green lentils. The taste will differ with regular hummus, but I bet you will like the sprouted hummus in Raw Food Feast if you are a hummus lover.

I recommend you soak the buckwheat and green lentils overnight; before starting the sprouting process. Buckwheat usually takes 1-2 days to sprout, and green lentils 4-5 days. Rinse the buckwheat and green lentils at least twice a day during the sprouting process (once in the morning and once in the evening is perfect).

Sunny soak water

I love to use sundried tomatoes in recipes because they add lots of flavor and body. For that nice salty flavor to recipes, I often use the soaking water of sundried tomatoes. I refer to it as sunny soak water in the recipes.

You can either use store-bought oil-free semi-sundried tomatoes or make your own. Usually, I keep a large jar of soaked sundried tomatoes in the fridge so that I have both sundried tomatoes as sunny soak water on hand at any given time.

I advise to soak the sundried tomatoes for at least eight hours in the water on the countertop. It creates both soft sundried tomatoes and that perfect salty sunny soak water.

Weight of ingredients

When a recipe calls for ¼ cup (45 g) buckwheat kernels, soaked and sprouted, I always refer to the weight before the soaking (and sprouting) process. The same goes for sundried tomatoes, nuts, seeds, and legumes. The reason is that the weight after soaking varies. The soaking time affects the weight and how much water the ingredients absorb.

When a recipe calls for ingredients to be soaked (and sprouted), it's included in the total inactive time it takes to create the recipe.

Dehydration time

Keep in mind that every dehydrator is different. It influences the total dehydration time called for in recipes, as well as the climate, does. Usually during warm days the process takes less time, and during colder days, it can take a bit more time.

The dehydration times are indications how long it takes on average when using a good quality dehydrator.

If you do not own a dehydrator but have an oven that warms at 105 °F/41 °C, then you can give the recipes that call for a dehydrator a try. Of course, the total time will differ when using an oven.

An oven is created to heat food, and a dehydrator to dry food, so an oven will take less time. Keep the door slightly open when you use an oven and check regularly how your wrap, bread, or burger is coming along.

One of the many benefits of owning a dehydrator is that you can use fruit and vegetables that are almost spoiled to create tasty foods, such as fruit leather or sundried tomatoes.

Green salt

I use salt sparingly, because of its effects. You can read more about the effects of salt on page 150, where you'll find the green salt recipe as well. Green salt is a great substitute for most types of salt without the negative effects salt has on the body.
Green salt, or any other salt, cannot be used as a substitute for black salt, also known as kala namak. The sulfur in kala namak adds an egg flavor to a recipe. Sometimes I add kala namak to a recipe to create that effect, but again I recommend using salt sparingly and choosing healthier options like green salt or sunny soak water instead.

Medjool dates

When a recipe calls for Medjool dates, they should be fresh and soft. If the Medjool dates aren't soft, soak them for about 30 minutes before use. It makes the blending process easier, but also creates a better structure when making a dressing, wrap, or soup base.

All sorts of recipes call for date paste. You can create your own, see page 156, or get it from the store. Date paste is not the same as date syrup, as date paste is fairly thick and date syrup is runny. However, both can be used to make the recipes.

Coconut vinegar

The reason why I prefer to use coconut vinegar over apple cider vinegar is that it's softer in taste and also slightly sweet. Plus, coconut vinegar contains all 9 essential amino acids.
If you don't have coconut vinegar on hand, you can, of course, replace it with apple cider vinegar, lime, or lemon juice. The taste will be slightly different though.

Mineral in abundance

Sea moss is a type of seaweed, a gift from the sea. It has many nutritional and medicinal benefits, and it's rich in fiber. It is said that sea moss contains quite the amount of minerals that our bodies require, iodine being one of them. Iodine is important for thyroid health.

There are all sorts of types of sea moss on the market, but I recommend that no matter which one you are getting, make sure it is always organically grown. I like sea moss gold the best.

I make sea moss gel at home from wildcrafted dehydrated sea moss. Besides the fact that it's a breeze to make sea moss gel, it's also very economical. You can make about 2500 ml sea moss gel from 150 grams of dried sea moss.

The only thing you have to do is wash and rinse the sea moss thoroughly, soak it with filtered water overnight, and blend with the soaking water in a high-speed blender until smooth. Next, add the gel to a jar and let it sit. It will firm up in an hour. You can store the gel in the fridge for up to two to three weeks. I usually soak about 30-50 grams per time and add per cup hydrated sea moss about half a cup of water. It is the consistency I like best for the gel.

If creating the raspberry chocolate mousse (page 135), you do not need to make a gel first. Just follow the instructions outlined in the recipe and blend the hydrated sea moss with the other listed ingredients to create the mousse. The other recipes using sea moss do call for sea moss gel.

Organic or conventional?

It is best to use organic produce when possible. For some, it might be challenging to get your hands on organic ingredients, and in other parts of the world, you pay quite a bit for it. Do what works best for you. If you are able to buy mostly organic produce, that's great. Make sure you always wash your produce before use, especially when the produce is not organic.

Cups and spoons

All the recipes call for US measuring cups and spoons. The benefit of using cups and spoons is that you have to weigh your ingredients less, which makes creating recipes easier. Need a cup of almond flour? Just scoop it with your cup and add it to the food processor. Easy like that. I recommend you get a set too, and you'll see how smoothly it works. It costs only a few dollars and is available at most cookware stores and online.

Happy uncooking!

I wish you health.
I wish you wealth
That passes not with time.
I wish you long years.
May your heart be as patient as the earth
Your love as warm as the harvest gold.
May your days be full, as the city is full
Your nights as joyful as dancers.
May your arms be as welcoming as home.
May your faith be as enduring as God's love
Your spirit as valiant as your heritage.
May your hand be as sure as a friend
Your dreams as hopeful as a child.
May your soul be as brave as your people
And may you be blessed.

- Wigglier Blessing

SMASHING SOUPS

souper power that makes you wanna dance

CREAMY CARROT SOUP

I like this soup best when it is chilled. So, regularly, as I make my juices and smoothies in the morning, I also juice some carrots to create this soup. Store the soup in the fridge for a few hours to enjoy it around lunchtime or dinner. Easy like that.

Active time 10 minutes | Makes 1 bowl of soup

INGREDIENTS

Creamy carrot soup base
1½ cups (355 ml) carrot juice
½ red bell pepper, chopped
½ avocado, chopped
1 tbsp lime juice
1 garlic clove, minced

Topping
1 spring onion stalk, thinly sliced
¼ tsp nigella seeds

METHOD

Blend the creamy carrot soup ingredients in a high-speed blender until smooth.

Pour the creamy carrot soup into a bowl and top with spring onion and nigella seeds.

RAW FOOD FEAST TIP
Use the carrot pulp to make crackers on page 72.

SWEET TOMATO SOUP

Are you in for a deliciously rich, bold, sweet tomato soup? It is your lucky day because here it is!
The dehydration process makes the flavors more intense, warms, and creates this beautiful thick sweet
tomato soup. If you want your soup to be ready in minutes, blend the soup for a couple of minutes in your
high-speed blender and add 1¼ cups of warm water instead of 1½ cups of water. Enjoy!

Active time 5-10 minutes | Inactive time 7 hours | Makes 1 bowl of soup

INGREDIENTS

1 large Roma tomato, chopped
4 sundried tomato halves, soaked
4 hours
½ red bell pepper, chopped
3 Medjool dates, pitted
1 tbsp pumpkin seeds
1 small garlic clove, minced
1 tsp dried Italian herbs
¼ tsp onion powder
1½ cups (355 ml) water

METHOD

Blend the sweet tomato soup ingredients in a high-speed blender
until smooth.

Pour the soup into a bowl and dehydrate for three hours at
115°F/46 °C.

VEGETABLE SOUP

This hearty vegetable soup is great after a long walk on the beach or a hike in nature. The nut balls give some extra body to the soup and the broth and veggies recharge your energy.

Active time 30 minutes | Inactive time 4 hours | Makes 1 bowl of soup

INGREDIENTS

Vegetable soup balls
¼ cup (30 g) almond flour
2 tbsp sunflower seeds, soaked 4 hours
1 tbsp chia seeds
1 tbsp psyllium husk powder
2 tbsp nutritional yeast
1 garlic clove, minced
¼ cup (60 ml) sunny soak water

Vegetable soup base
1 celery stalk, chopped
1 Medjool date, pitted
1 garlic clove, minced
1 tsp onion powder
1 tsp garlic powder
¼ tsp dried oregano
¼ tsp chili flakes
1½ cups (355 ml) water
½ cup (120 ml) sunny soak water

Vegetable soup ingredients
1 handful bok choi, finely chopped
1 celery stalk, finely chopped
1 medium carrot, finely chopped

METHOD

Blend the vegetable soup balls ingredients in a high-speed blender into a smooth dough.

Divide the dough into 12 equal portions, create the soup balls, and set aside.

Blend the vegetable soup base ingredients in a high-speed blender until smooth and warm.

In the meantime, prepare the vegetable soup ingredients.

Add the soup ingredients and balls into a bowl and add the vegetable soup base.

CORN CHOWDER SOUP

Corn chowder is a soft and slightly sweet soup.
Dip some buckwheat bread in your soup and serve it with a big salad to enjoy a beautiful meal.

Active time 10 minutes | Makes 1 bowl of soup

INGREDIENTS

Corn chowder soup base
½ cup (50 g) young coconut meat
1 cup (140 g) corn kernels
½ cup (75 g) sweet potato, chopped
1 celery stalk, chopped
1 garlic clove, minced
1 tsp onion powder
1 tsp garlic powder
½ tsp sweet paprika powder
½ tsp dried thyme
½ cup (120 ml) sunny soak water
½ cup (120 ml) water

Topping
corn kernels to taste
chili flakes to taste
garlic croutons to taste, page 147
(optional)

METHOD

Blend the corn chowder soup ingredients in a high-speed blender until smooth and warm.

Pour the corn chowder soup into a bowl and top with corn kernels, chili flakes, and optionally garlic croutons.

MINESTRONE SOUP

If you prefer to add soft veggies to your soup, freeze the bell pepper, carrot, and celery overnight and thaw. The freezing process will soften your veggies without losing flavor, enzymes, and nutrients.

Active time 15 minutes | Makes 1 bowl of soup

INGREDIENTS

Minestrone soup base
1 medium carrot, chopped
4 Roma tomatoes, chopped
2 Medjool dates, pitted
1 garlic clove, minced
1 tsp dried parsley
1 tsp onion powder
½ cup (120 ml) water

Minestrone ingredients
¼ zucchini, spiralized
1 Roma tomato, chopped
¼ red bell pepper, chopped
1 medium carrot, chopped
1 celery stalk, chopped

Topping
spring onion to taste
dried parsley to taste
chili flakes to taste

METHOD

Blend the minestrone soup base ingredients in a high-speed blender until smooth and warm.

In the meantime, prepare the minestrone ingredients.

Add the minestrone ingredients into a bowl, add the minestrone soup base, and top with spring onion, dried parsley, and chili flakes.

BANGER SALADS

saladbrate good times!

FUSION NOODLE SALAD

Confession time: to show you more than just a glimpse of the fusion noodle salad, I had to withhold myself not to pile it with cilantro leaves. If you are also a massive cilantro lover, don't let anything or anyone stop you from burying your fusion noodle salad with this delicious, healthy herb.

Active time 25-30 minutes | Inactive time 8 hours | Makes 2 salads

INGREDIENTS

Fusion dressing
1 cup (120 g) cashew nuts, soaked 8 hours
½ cup (120 ml) sunny soak water
2 tbsp coconut vinegar
4 tbsp date paste
2 tbsp tahini
2 tbsp ginger, grated
2 garlic cloves, minced
2 tsp curry powder
1 tbsp sesame seeds

Noodle salad
12 oz/340 g kelp noodles
5 oz/150 g iceberg lettuce, finely chopped
6 oz/180 g red cabbage, thinly sliced
1 cucumber, spiralized
1 large carrot, julienne cut
1 yellow bell pepper, thinly sliced

Topping
bean sprouts to taste
spring onion to taste
cilantro leaves to taste

METHOD

Blend the fusion dressing ingredients, except the sesame seeds, in a high-speed blender until smooth.

In the meantime, rinse the kelp noodles thoroughly, pet dry, and add to a large bowl.

Stir the sesame seeds into the fusion dressing.

Pour half of the fusion dressing on the kelp noodles and combine well.

Prepare the remaining noodle salad ingredients, add to the kelp noodles, and combine well.

Add the rest of the dressing to the fusion noodle salad and top with bean sprouts, spring onion, and (lots of) cilantro.

CHIPOTLE RANCH SALAD

Lamb's lettuce is one of my favorite greens to create a salad, besides Romaine lettuce.
I've found that lamb's lettuce tends to splash the dressing because of its beautiful shape. Cut the lamb's lettuce with a scissor into smaller pieces to make it easier to eat and prevent splashing.

Active time 20 minutes | Inactive time 4 hours | Makes 2 salads

INGREDIENTS

Chipotle ranch dressing
½ cup (60 g) sunflower seeds, soaked 4 hours
½ cup (60 g) zucchini, chopped
1 Medjool date, pitted
1 tbsp lime juice
1 small garlic clove, minced
½ tsp chipotle powder
½ tsp mustard powder
1 tsp onion powder
¾ cup (180 ml) sunny soak water
2 tbsp dill leaves, finely cut

Salad
7 oz/200 g lamb's lettuce
½ portion marinated carrots (page 148)
20 mini Roma tomatoes, chopped
1 cucumber, matchsticks
1 cup (140 g) pineapple, finely chopped
1 avocado, finely chopped
1 cup (140 g) pickles, finely chopped

Topping
sprouts of choice to taste
¼ cup (40 g) dried cranberries
spring onion to taste

METHOD

Blend the chipotle ranch dressing ingredients, except for the dill leaves, in a high-speed blender until smooth.

In the meantime, prepare the salad ingredients, add to a large bowl, except for the lamb's lettuce, and combine well.

Stir the dill leaves into the chipotle ranch dressing.

Mix the lamb's lettuce with the chipotle ranch dressing.

Combine the lamb's lettuce with the other salad ingredients and top with sprouts, cranberries, and spring onion.

KIMCHI CUCUMBER SALAD

I don't know about you, but the first time I tasted kimchi, I fell in love right away, much to the surprise of my Korean friends. The tangy, sour, yet fresh flavors bring it home for me.
This kimchi cucumber salad is a perfect spicy side dish.

Active time 30 minutes | Inactive time 8 hours | Makes 5-6 portions

INGREDIENTS

Salad
35 oz/1 kg mini cucumbers, unpeeled and chopped
1 tbsp green salt
3 spring onion stalks, finely chopped
1-2 green rawit pepper, finely chopped

Kimchi dressing
¼ avocado
2 tbsp date paste
1 tbsp chili flakes
1 tsp onion powder
1 garlic clove, minced
¼ cup (60 ml) coconut vinegar
¼ cup (60 ml) water
1 tbsp sesame seeds

Topping
spring onion to taste
sesame seeds to taste
chili flakes to taste

METHOD

Add the cucumber and green salt to a large bowl, coat the pieces equally, and set aside for about 10 minutes to draw out the moisture.

Blend the kimchi dressing ingredients, except the sesame seeds, in a high-speed blender until smooth.

In the meantime, prepare the spring onion and rawit pepper, and add it to a large bowl.

Stir the sesame seeds into the kimchi dressing.

Gently press the cucumber to drain excess liquid and add to the spring onion and pepper.

Pour the dressing on top of the salad ingredients and combine well.

Marinate the kimchi cucumber salad for 8 hours in the fridge.

RAW FOOD FEAST TIP
If you do not have green salt on your hands, you can use Himalaya or Celtic sea salt instead. Use ½ tsp to draw out the moisture.
Give the cucumbers a quick rinse and pat them dry to remove the remains of the salt.

CREAMY BEET SALAD

Raw beet is a powerhouse. It is full of crucial nutrients and a blessing for the kidneys because of its cleansing effect. Pure beet juice is also delicious. However, if you're not yet used to the power of beetroot, then build up drinking pure beet juice. Combining beet juice with freshly pressed carrot and ginger juice is divine.

Active time 15-20 minutes | Makes 1 salad

INGREDIENTS

Beet tahini dressing
1 cup (150 g) red beet, chopped
3 Medjool dates, pitted
¼ cup (60 ml) tahini
¼ cup (60 ml) sunny soak water
¼ cup (60 ml) water

Salad
1 head of Romaine lettuce, chopped
1 orange bell pepper, finely chopped
1 yellow bell pepper, finely chopped
12 cherry tomatoes, in halves
3 radish, finely chopped
½ avocado, chopped
3 spring onion stalks, finely chopped

METHOD

Blend the beet tahini dressing ingredients in a high-speed blender until smooth.

In the meantime, prepare the salad, add to a large bowl, and combine well.

Pour the beet tahini dressing on top of the salad.

Enjoy!

CAESAR SALAD

Caesar salad is known for its simplicity and deliciousness. Romaine lettuce is such a healthy green. Its nutritional value is off the charts. Romaine lettuce comes in many sizes, but don't be shy to use a nice big head of Romaine lettuce to build your salad. Enjoy!

Active time 15 minutes | Inactive time 3-5 hours | Makes 1 salad

INGREDIENTS

Caesar dressing
½ cup (60 g) hulled hemp seeds
½ cup (120 ml) water
½ tbsp Dijon mustard
¼ cup (15 g) nutritional yeast
1 tbsp capers
1 tbsp lime juice
1 garlic clove, minced
1 tsp onion powder
½ tsp garlic powder

Salad
1 head of Romaine lettuce, chopped

Topping
garlic croutons to taste, page 147
parsley to taste, finely chopped
capers to taste
nutritional yeast to taste

METHOD

Create the garlic croutons ahead of time.

Blend the Caesar dressing ingredients in a high-speed blender until smooth.

In the meantime, chop the Romaine lettuce and add it to a large bowl.

Pour the Caesar dressing on the Romaine lettuce, mix well, and add the toppings.

THOUSAND ISLAND SALAD

In my opinion, pretty much any salad is a joy to eat. But certain dressings are so good that they make your salad top-notch. Thousand island dressing falls into that category. It's creamy, rich, and fresh.
Adding beautiful flavor and body to your salad, making it satiating and a party for your taste buds.

Active time 15-20 minutes | Inactive time 8 hours | Makes 2 salads

INGREDIENTS

Thousand island dressing
¼ cup (30 g) cashew nuts, soaked 8 hours
½ cup (40 g) sundried tomatoes, soaked 8 hours
1½ cups (355 ml) orange juice
1 Medjool date, pitted
½ cup (70 g) pickles, finely chopped
1 spring onion stalk
½ tsp paprika powder
¼ tsp mustard powder

Salad
7 oz/200 g spinach, chopped
20 mini Roma tomatoes, halves
1 cucumber, finely chopped
2 mangoes, finely chopped
2 orange bell peppers, finely chopped
1 avocado, chopped
1 cup (140 g) pickles, finely chopped

Topping
spring onion to taste

METHOD

Blend the thousand island dressing ingredients, except for a ¼ cup pickles, in a high-speed blender until smooth.

In the meantime, prepare the salad, add to a large bowl, and combine well.

Stir the pickles into the thousand island dressing.

Pour the thousand island dressing on top of the salad, grab a fork and dig in.

TANGY TAHINI SALAD

Tangy tahini dressing is slightly addictive.
Pour it onto your salad or straight into your mouth. It's that good.

Active time 15-20 minutes | Makes 1 salad

INGREDIENTS

Tangy tahini dressing
4 Medjool dates, pitted
¼ cup (60 ml) tahini
¼ cup (60 ml) lime juice
½ jalapeno, chopped
1 tbsp nutritional yeast
½ cup (120 ml) water

Salad
1 head of Romaine lettuce, chopped
1 mango, finely chopped
½ cup (100 g) fennel, finely chopped
10 Roma tomatoes, quartered
5 mini cucumbers or ½ cucumber, sliced
3 radish, sliced

Topping
peppadew pepper to taste, thinly sliced
spring onion to taste

METHOD

Blend the tangy tahini dressing ingredients in a high-speed blender until smooth.

In the meantime, prepare the salad, add to a large bowl, and combine well.

Pour the tangy tahini dressing on top of the salad and top with peppadew peppers and spring onion.

RAW FOOD FEAST TIP
Peppadew peppers are usually found in the same aisle as pickles or condiments. They add a little kick to any dish. You can use pickles instead but the taste will differ.

SHAVED BRUSSELS SPROUTS SALAD

Shaved Brussels sprouts salad is perfect as a side dish. It's easy to make, healthy, and satiating.

Active time 25-30 minutes | Makes 5-6 portions

INGREDIENTS

Salad ingredients
17.5 oz/500 g Brussels sprouts, shaved
5 oz/150 g red cabbage, thinly sliced
1 big Granny Smith apple, finely chopped
2 tbsp lime juice
¼ cup (25 g) pomegranate seeds
¼ cup (25 g) slivered almonds
½ cup (60 g) pecan nuts, chopped
½ cup (80 g) dried cranberries

Marinade
1 cup (235 ml) blood orange juice
2 tbsp balsamico cream

METHOD

Prepare the salad ingredients and add to a large bowl.

Add the marinade ingredients to a small bowl and whisk until combined.

Pour the marinade on top of the shaved Brussels sprouts salad and mix well.

FUNKY BITES

bites to the beat of your own drum

CROSTINI

Do you want some gluten-free and healthy breadsticks to dip in your soup or munch? Here you go!
I love the taste of nigella seeds. It's also known as black cumin. If you don't have nigella seeds, you can
use sesame seeds to top your crostini.

Active time 20-30 minutes | Inactive time 2-3 days | Makes 8 crostini

INGREDIENTS

Crostini ingredients
½ cup (90 g) buckwheat kernels,
soaked and sprouted
½ cup (50 g) blond flax meal
2 tbsp nutritional yeast
1 tbsp psyllium husk powder
2 sundried tomato halves, soaked
4 hours
leaves of 1 rosemary sprig
2 tbsp sunny soak water

Topping
nigella seeds to taste

METHOD

Add the crostini ingredients to a food processor and mix them
into a dough.

Divide the dough into eight equal parts and create sticks about
½"/1 cm thick.

Lightly wet one crostini at a time on both sides and sprinkle with
nigella seeds.

Press the nigella seeds into the dough.

Carefully twist the crostini.

Dehydrate the crostini first at 145 °F/63 °C for two hours and then
for another 6-8 hours at 115 °F/46 °C.

The crostini should be completely dry.

RAW FOOD FEAST TIP
This dough is pretty dry. Work both with warm hands and quickly
for the best result. Lightly wetting the crostini on both sides before
creating the twist prevents breaking.

CUCUMBER ROLL-UPS

These fresh and healthy cucumber roll-ups are the perfect finger food to serve at a party.
Cucumber roll-ups are easy to make, look gorgeous, and taste scrumptious.

Active time 15-20 minutes | Inactive time 16-20 hours | Makes 7 roll-ups

INGREDIENTS

1 large cucumber, strips
2-3 tbsp balsamic onion spread,
page 118
2 handsful arugula
¼ portion marinated carrots,
page 148
¼ avocado, sliced
sprouts of choice to taste
dill leaves to taste

METHOD

Make the balsamic onion spread ahead of time.

Place the cucumber strips next to each other on a bleach-free paper towel on a flat surface, such as a cutting board. Be sure the cucumber strips overlap to keep them together when rolling and cutting into roll-ups. Place another paper towel on top of the cucumber strips and pat dry.

Spread the balsamic onion spread evenly onto the cucumber strips.

Add the arugula, marinated carrots, avocado, and sprouts. Keep the top and bottom free, like when making a sushi roll.

Carefully roll the cucumber strips into a roll.

Cut the cucumber roll with a sharp knife into seven equal slices.

Top the cucumber roll-ups with dill leaves.

RAW FOOD FEAST TIP
Use the left-over cucumber to dip with sprouted lentil hummus,
page 121 or add to a salad.

BEET CARPACCIO

This beet carpaccio is a perfect starter when enjoying dinner with loved ones.
Also, both the almond crumble cheese and lime poppy seed dressing are great to add to a salad.

Active time 40 minutes | Inactive time 12 hours | Makes 4 carpaccios

INGREDIENTS

Almond crumble cheese
½ cup (60 g) almonds, soaked
8 hours
2 tbsp lime juice
1 tbsp green salt
1 garlic clove, minced
½ cup (120 ml) sunny soak water

Lime poppy seed dressing
½ cup (120 ml) lime juice
6 Medjool dates, pitted
2 tsp poppy seeds
2 tsp Dijon mustard
2 tsp ginger, grated
1 large garlic clove, minced
½ cup (120 ml) water

Carpaccio
6 medium beets, very thinly sliced
4 handsful arugula
2-3 tbsp capers

METHOD

After soaking, skin the almonds. Simply pinch one end of the almond to loosen the skin.

Blend the almond crumble cheese ingredients in a high-speed blender until smooth.

Scoop the almond crumble cheese into a nut milk bag or cheese-cloth and drain its liquid.

Place the nut milk bag in a bowl and add weight to it. Let it sit for four hours or overnight.

Blend the lime poppy seed dressing ingredients in a high-speed blender until smooth.

Remove the almond crumble cheese from the nut milk bag and carefully crumble the cheese.

Place the beet slices in a flower shape on four plates, add the lime poppy seed dressing, arugula, and capers.

RAW FOOD FEAST TIP
Use a mandoline or food processor to slice the beets.

PLANTAIN PANCAKES

Plantain pancakes are the answer if you love a hearty breakfast or a delicous brunch.

Active time 10-15 minutes | Inactive time 4-5 hours | Makes 8 pancakes

INGREDIENTS

Plantain pancakes
2 plantain
1 tbsp psyllium husk powder
1 tbsp coconut aminos
½ tbsp cardamom powder
½ tbsp cinnamon powder
1 cup (235 ml) water

Topping
berries of choice to taste
coconut flakes to taste
date syrup to taste

METHOD

Blend the plantain pancakes ingredients in a high-speed blender into a smooth batter.

Divide the batter into eight equal parts and spread evenly onto a non-stick dehydrator sheet, about ¼"/0,5 cm thick.

Create the plantain pancakes with your hands or a spatula.
If you prefer to use a cooking ring to create pancakes, then Ø 4"/10 cm is a perfect size.

Dehydrate the pancakes at 115 °F/46 °C for two hours.

Flip the pancakes onto other dehydrator trays and carefully remove the non-stick sheets.

Dehydrate the pancakes for another 2-3 hours at 115 °F/46 °C.

The pancakes should be soft and pliable.

Stack the plantain pancakes, drizzle with date syrup, and top with berries and coconut flakes.

RAW FOOD FEAST TIP
Use very ripe plantain for the best pancakes.

RAWNOLA BALLS

Rawnola balls are the perfect pick-me-up when in need of energy and deliciousness.

Active time 20-25 minutes | Inactive time 2-3 days | Makes 25 balls

INGREDIENTS

Rawnola filling
½ cup (90 g) buckwheat kernels, soaked and sprouted
½ cup (70 g) pumpkin seeds, soaked 4 hours
½ cup (60 g) hulled hemp seeds
2 tbsp cranberries
2 tbsp raisins

Rawnola bar
¼ cup (25 g) young coconut meat
8 Medjool dates, pitted
2 tbsp psyllium husk powder
½ tbsp cardamom powder
½ tbsp carob powder
2-4 tbsp water

METHOD

Blend the rawnola balls ingredients in a high-speed blender until smooth.

In the meantime, add the rawnola filling ingredients into a bowl and mix well.

Add the rawnola balls ingredients to the bowl, combine well, and chill in the fridge for at least 8 hours.

Divide the rawnola mixture into 25 equal parts and form balls.

Store the rawnola balls in an air-tight container in the fridge.

INDIAN TORTILLA CHIPS

Serve these crunchy Indian tortilla chips with pico de gallo, artichoke spinach dip (page 128), and create a delicious raw food platter to share with loved ones.

Active time 45 minutes | Inactive time 15 hours | Makes 8-12 portions

INGREDIENTS

4 cups (560 g) corn kernels
1 cup (235 ml) coconut water
1 cup (150 g) blond flax seeds,
soaked 1 hour
½ cup (120 ml) sunny soak water
to soak the flax seeds
½ cup (50 g) young coconut meat
½ cup (20 g) cilantro, stems and
leaves, tightly packed
1 tbsp psyllium husk powder
1 tbsp lime juice
2 tbsp green salt
2 tsp cumin powder
1 tsp chili flakes

Topping
nigella seeds to taste

METHOD

Add the ingredients to a food processor and mix them into a smooth dough.

Divide the dough into five equal parts and spread evenly onto five non-stick dehydrator sheets, about 1/8"/0,3 cm thick.

Top the dough with nigella seeds and score the dough into rounds, squares, or triangles.

Dehydrate the chips at 145 °F/63 °C for two hours.

Flip the chips onto other dehydrator trays and carefully remove the non-stick sheets.

Dehydrate the chips for another 12 hours at 115 °F/46 °C.

The Indian tortilla chips should be dry and crunchy.

RUTABAGA FRIES

The freezing process softens the rutabaga (or any other vegetable), giving it an al dente texture. Rutabaga fries with a bite are its result. You can also freeze the rutabaga fries overnight.

Active time 5-10 minutes | Inactive time 9 hour | Makes 4 portions

INGREDIENTS

28 oz/800 g rutabaga, sticks
1 tbsp green salt
1 tbsp chili flakes

METHOD

Freeze the rutabaga fries for four hours and let them thaw.

Pet the rutabaga fries dry, add green salt and chili flakes and combine well.

Spread the rutabaga fries evenly onto two dehydrator trays.

Dehydrate the rutabaga fries at 105 °F/41 °C for one hour.

Serve the rutabaga fries with a sauce of your choice.

PARTY CRACKERS

gut feeling good bread, bagels, crackers, and wraps

BELL PEPPER DATE WRAPS

Let's create some salad wrapped in disguise because that's what a good wrap is, right?!
These easy-to-make bell pepper date wraps are downright delicious. I make wraps regularly as they are perfect for lunch, dinner, or on the go. Beach day or picnic in the park? Make wraps and bring them along. These wraps don't get soggy when prepared in advance.

Active time 20-30 minutes | Inactive time 6-8 hours | Makes 2 wraps

INGREDIENTS

17.5 oz/500 g red bell pepper
3 Medjool dates, pitted
1 tsp za'atar
1 tbsp sea moss gel
2 tbsp blond flax meal
1 tbsp psyllium husk powder
½ cup (120 ml) sunny soak water

METHOD

Add the ingredients to a food processor and mix them into a smooth dough.

Divide the dough into two equal parts and spread evenly onto two non-stick dehydrator sheets, about ¼"/0,5 cm thick.

Create the wraps with your hands or a spatula.

Dehydrate the wraps at 145 °F/63 °C for two hours.

Flip the wraps onto other dehydrator trays and carefully remove the non-stick sheets.

Dehydrate the wraps for another 3-5 hours at 115 °F/46 °C.

The bell pepper date wraps should be pretty dry and pliable.

RAW FOOD FEAST TIP
Lightly wet your hands to form the wraps with ease.

BUCKWHEAT BREAD

Most bread is harmful to your gut because it acts like glue. Over time your digestive system won't be able to absorb the nutrients, and you are left with deficiencies, to name a few of the downsides of bread. But no worries. You can enjoy the most delicious raw bread that is healthy, satiating, and a breeze to make. Let's unbake some!

Active time 10-15 minutes | Inactive time 3-4 days | Makes 1 loaf of bread

INGREDIENTS

1 cup (180 g) buckwheat kernels, soaked and sprouted
¾ cup (115 g) chia seeds, soaked overnight
1 cup (235 ml) water to soak the chia seeds
½ cup (50 g) blond flax meal
2 tbsp sea moss gel
1 tbsp carraway seeds
1 tsp onion powder
1 tsp garlic powder
¼ cup (60 ml) sunny soak water

METHOD

Add the ingredients to a food processor and mix them into a dough.

Lightly wet your hands and create a loaf of bread to your liking.

Dehydrate the buckwheat bread first at 145 °F/63 °C for two hours and then for another 8-10 hours at 115 °F/46 °C.

The buckwheat bread should be pretty dry on the outside but soft on the inside.

PULP CRACKERS

If you are into juicing and you wonder what to do with the pulp, here is the answer: create crackers. This recipes calls for carrot pulp, but feel free to experiment with pulp from other veggies and greens.

Active time 20-30 minutes | Inactive time 15-17 hours | Makes 16 crackers

INGREDIENTS

1 cup (150 g) blond flax seeds, soaked 1 hour
½ cup (120 ml) sunny soak water to soak the flax seeds
1½ cups (150 g) carrot pulp
¼ cup (20 g) sundried tomatoes, soaked 8 hours
½ cup (50 g) blond flax meal
1 tbsp sea moss gel
1 tsp onion powder
1 tsp garlic clove, minced
½ cup (120 ml) water

METHOD

Add the ingredients, except for the blond flax seeds, to a food processor and mix them into a dough.

Stir in the blond flax seeds and combine well with a spatula.

Divide the dough into two equal parts and spread evenly onto two non-stick dehydrator sheets, about ¼"/0,5 cm thick.

Score the dough into eight equal pieces.

Dehydrate the pulp crackers at 145 °F/63 °C for two hours.

Flip the crackers onto other dehydrator trays and carefully remove the non-stick sheets.

Dehydrate the crackers for another 4-6 hours at 115 °F/46 °C.

The pulp crackers should be dry and crunchy.

ZA'ATAR FLATBREAD

Za'atar flatbread is simply amazing. You can add any spread and toppings to create your favorite flatbread for lunch or dinner with a healthy salad on the side.

Active time 30 minutes | Inactive time 7-9 hours | Makes 8 flatbreads

INGREDIENTS

1 cup (120 g) almond flour
½ cup (70 g) quinoa flour
½ cup (60 g) hulled hemp seeds
½ cup (50 g) blond flax meal
1 cup (170 g) dried figs
5 oz/150 g cucumber, chopped
1 tbsp za'atar
2 tbsp onion powder
1 large garlic clove, minced
1 tbsp psyllium husk powder
1 tbsp chia seeds
1½ cup (355 ml) sunny soak water

METHOD

Add the ingredients to a food processor and mix them into a dough.

Divide the dough into two equal parts and spread evenly onto two non-stick dehydrator sheets, about ¼"/0,5 cm thick.

Create the flatbreads with your hands or a spatula.

Score the dough into four equal pieces.

Dehydrate the flatbreads at 145 °F/63 °C for two hours.

Flip the flatbreads onto other dehydrator trays and carefully remove the non-stick sheets.

Dehydrate the flatbread for another 4-6 hours at 115 °F/46 °C.

The za'atar flatbread should be dry and pliable.

RAW FOOD FEAST TIP
Lightly wet your hands to form the flatbread with ease.

SPROUTED ALMOND BAGELS

Whose doesn't love a good bagel from time to time? Serve with dill caper cashew cream (page 122), arugula, marinated carrots (page 148), capers, sprouts, and top with fresh dill. Enjoy!

Active time 30 minutes | Inactive time 3-4 days | Makes 4 bagels

INGREDIENTS

1 cup (180 g) buckwheat kernels, soaked and sprouted
½ cup (60 g) almond flour
5 oz/150 g zucchini, chopped
1 tbsp chia seeds
2 tbsp psyllium husk powder
2 tsp onion powder
1 tsp dried oregano
1 cup (235 ml) sunny soak water

METHOD

Add the ingredients to a food processor and mix them into a dough.

Divide the dough into four equal parts.

Lightly wet your hands, and create bagels.

Dehydrate the sprouted almond bagels first at 145 °F/63 °C for two hours and then for another 6-8 hours at 115 °F/46 °C.

The sprouted almond bagels should be pretty dry on the outside and soft on the inside.

MEDITERRANEAN BREADSTICKS

Even though the word 'wheat' pops up in buckwheat, it's not wheat but a seed instead. Buckwheat is gluten-free and loaded with fiber. Glady, we hear more and more about the importance of fiber.
Even though fiber is not a nutrient for your cells, it's fuel to your gut microbiome.
Your gut plays a vital role in your overall health, as a big part of your immune system will weaken or strengthen by the condition of your gut microbiome. Happy gut, happy you.

Active time 20-30 minutes | Inactive time 3 days | Makes 24 breadsticks

INGREDIENTS

½ cup (90 g) buckwheat kernels, soaked and sprouted
½ cup (75 g) blond flax seeds
¼ cup (60 ml) water
5 oz/150 g zucchini, chopped
½ cup (40 g) sundried tomatoes, soaked 4 hours
2 tbsp psyllium husk powder
2 tbsp blond flax meal
1 tsp onion powder
1 tsp garlic powder
½ cup (120 ml) sunny soak water
¼ cup (40 g) sundried olives, sliced

METHOD

Add the ingredients, except the sundried olives, to a food processor and mix them into a dough.

In the meantime, prepare the olives.

Stir the olives into the dough and combine well.

Divide the dough into four equal parts.

Lightly wet your hands and create bread slices, about ½"/1 cm thick.

Place the bread slices onto a non-stick dehydrator sheet and dehydrate at 145 °F/63 °C for two hours.

Flip the bread slices onto another dehydrator tray, and carefully remove the non-stick sheet.

Dehydrate the bread slices for another 6-8 hours at 115°F/46 °C.

After four hours remove the bread slices from the dehydrator and cut them into sticks.

Put the breadsticks back into the dehydrator and dehydrate until the slices are pretty dry and pliable.

RAW FOOD FEAST IDEA
Serve these delicious Mediterranean breadsticks with oil-free pesto, caperberries, peppadew peppers, sundried olives, and non-sweet fruits, like cherry tomatoes and mini bell peppers.

SUNDRIED TOMATO CRACKERS

These tasty sundried tomato crackers are a great add-on to any raw food platter. Add a little spread, for example sprouted lentil hummus (page 121), some pickled red onions (page 144), and crunchy sprouts, and let your teeth sink into that goodness. It's simple as that. Let's make some!

Active time 20-30 minutes | Inactive time 14-16 hours | Makes about 48 crackers

INGREDIENTS

1 cup (120 g) sunflower seeds, soaked 4 hours
1 cup (80 g) sundried tomatoes, soaked 8 hours
½ cup (50 g) blond flax meal
½ cup (20 g) parsley, stems and leaves, tightly packed
1 tsp green salt
1 tsp dried oregano
1 tsp onion powder
1 garlic clove, minced
1 tbsp sea moss gel
½ cup (120 ml) water

METHOD

Add the ingredients to a food processor and mix them into a dough.

Divide the dough into two equal parts and spread evenly onto two non-stick dehydrator sheets, about ¼"/0,5 cm thick.

Create the crackers with your hands or a spatula.

Score the dough into equal square pieces.

Dehydrate the crackers at 145 °F/63 °C for two hours.

Flip the crackers onto other dehydrator trays and carefully remove the non-stick sheets.

Dehydrate the crackers for another 4-6 hours at 115 °F/46 °C.

The sundried tomato crackers should be dry and crunchy.

GREEN PEA WRAPS

These green pea wraps are heavenly. Serve with dill caper cashew cream (page 122), lamb's lettuce, avocado, oil-free sundried tomatoes, mint leaves, sprouts, and top with pickled red onions (page 144).

Active time 20-30 minutes | Inactive time 6-8 hours | Makes 4 wraps

INGREDIENTS

1 cup (140 g) green peas
0.9 oz/25 g spinach
3.5 oz/100 g tomato, diced
¼ cup (25 g) blond flax meal
2 tbsp pine nuts
1 tbsp nutritional yeast
2 tbsp chives, chopped
1 tbsp psyllium husk powder
½ cup (120 ml) sunny soak water

METHOD

Add the ingredients to a food processor and mix them into a smooth dough.

Divide the dough into four equal parts and spread evenly onto two non-stick dehydrator sheets, about ¼"/0,5 cm thick.

Create the wraps with your hands or a spatula.

Dehydrate the wraps at 145 °F/63 °C for two hours.

Flip the wraps onto other dehydrator trays and carefully remove the non-stick sheets.

Dehydrate the wraps for another 3-5 hours at 115 °F/46 °C.

The wraps should be dry and pliable.

RAW FOOD FEAST TIP
Lightly wet your hands to form the wraps with ease.

TAKE ME TO THE BALL

balls, burgers, and all that jazz

SPROUTED LENTIL BURGER

Are you looking for a burger that is both delicious and a blessing to your gut microbiome? Look no further because you have come to the right place! Sprouted green lentils are full of fiber, vitamin C, and zink. Zink supports immune function, aids in regulating enzyme activity, and acts as an impressive free-radical fighter, to name a few. Happy sprouting!

Active time 20-30 minutes | Inactive time 9-11 hours | Makes 4 patties

INGREDIENTS

¼ cup (50 g) green lentils, soaked and sprouted (yields 2 cups)
3.5 oz/100 g zucchini, chopped
½ cup (20 g) parsley, stems and leaves, tightly packed
½ cup (40 g) sundried tomatoes, soaked 8 hours
¼ cup + 2 tbsp (45 g) almond flour
¼ cup (15 g) nutritional yeast
¼ avocado
2 tbsp tahini
2 garlic cloves, minced
1 tsp curry powder
¼ tsp chipotle powder
1 tsp dried oregano
1 tbsp psyllium husk powder
½ cup (120 ml) sunny soak water

METHOD

Add the ingredients to a food processor and mix them until well combined.

Divide the mixture into four equal parts, create burgers to your liking, and place them onto a non-stick dehydrator sheet.

Dehydrate the burgers at 145 °F/63 °C for two hours.

Flip the burgers onto another dehydrator tray and carefully remove the non-stick sheet.

Dehydrate the burgers for another 3-5 hours at 115 °F/46 °C.

The sprouted lentil burgers should be dry on the outside and slightly soft on the inside.

RAW FOOD FEAST TIP
If you like smaller patties, divide the mixture into six equal parts. Adjust dehydration time accordingly.

JACKFRUIT BURGER

Young jackfruit is so versatile because of its neutral taste. You can marinade young jackfruit with any sauce you enjoy to create all sorts of deliciousness. Use lettuce of your choice as a bun and add any toppings and sauce you like to build your favorite jackfruit burger.

Active time 15 minutes | Inactive time 2 hours | Makes 2 portions

INGREDIENTS

20 oz/565 g shredded young jackfruit, thoroughly drained

Shiitake marinade
½ cup (120 ml) water
3 shiitake, chopped
2 Medjool dates, pitted
2 tbsp tahini
1 garlic clove, minced
½ tbsp chili flakes
2 tsp lime juice

METHOD

Blend the shiitake marinade ingredients in a high-speed blender until smooth.

Remove any hard young jackfruit pieces.

Add the jackfruit and marinade in a bowl and combine well.

Spread the marinated jackfruit evenly onto a non-stick dehydrator sheet.

Dehydrate the jackfruit at 105 °F/41 °C for two hours.

Build your burger and let your teeth sink in!

FALAFEL

If you want to set your teeth in the best falafel ever: you've come to the right recipe!
The falafel tastes great by itself, but you can add them to salads, wraps, or on top of a slice of buckwheat
bread (page 70), for example. Whatever you fancy.

Active time 25-30 minutes | Inactive time 13-15 hours | Makes 16 falafel

INGREDIENTS

¼ cup (50 g) green lentils, soaked and sprouted*
¼ cup + 2 tbsp (15 g) cilantro, stems and leaves, tightly packed
½ cup (40 g) sundried tomatoes, soaked 8 hours
¼ cup (30 g) almond flour
1 tbsp psyllium husk powder
¼ cup (60 ml) tahini
1 garlic clove, minced
2 tbsp lime juice
1 tsp cumin powder
¼ tsp chipotle powder
1 tbsp green salt
½ cup (120 ml) sunny soak water

METHOD

Add the ingredients to a food processor and mix them into a smooth dough.

Divide the dough into 16 equal parts and create balls.

Place the falafel onto a non-stick dehydrator sheet.

Dehydrate the falafel at 145 °F/ 63 °C for two hours.

Flip the falafel onto another dehydrator sheet and carefully remove the silicon sheet.

Dehydrate the falafel for another 3-5 hours at 115 °F/ 46 °C.

*1/4 cup green lentils gives about two cups of sprouts.

GARDEN BURGER

Seriously, you don't need to miss out on anything when you embrace a (high) raw food lifestyle.
The garden burger is pure bliss. Serve on an iceberg lettuce bun with
tomato, cucumber, pickled red onions (page 144), and sweet barbecue sauce (page 116).

Active time 30 minutes | Inactive time 13-15 hours | Makes 4 patties

INGREDIENTS

1½ cups (210 g) corn kernels
½ cup (70 g) carrot, chopped
½ cup (70 g) red bell pepper, chopped
¼ cup (20 g) sundried tomatoes, soaked 8 hours
1 celery stalk, roughly chopped
½ cup (20 g) cilantro, stems and leaves, tightly packed
1 tbsp psyllium husk powder
1 tbsp chia seeds
1 tsp dried oregano
1 tsp dried thyme
1 tsp garlic powder
1 tsp onion powder

METHOD

Add the ingredients to a food processor and mix them until well combined.

Divide the mixture into four equal parts, create burgers to your liking, and place them onto a non-stick dehydrator sheet.

Dehydrate the burgers at 145 °F/63 °C for two hours.

Flip the burgers onto another dehydrator tray and carefully remove the non-stick sheet.

Dehydrate the burgers for another 3-5 hours at 115 °F/46 °C.

The garden burger should be dry on the outside and soft on the inside.

MANCHURIAN

This recipe calls to be doubled. No, wait: tripled. I don't know about you, but I find that working with my hands with food is a form of meditation, or as some like to call it: therapeutic. I hope you enjoy your meditation session, and even more, to set your teeth into this spicy deliciousness.

Active time 45 minutes | Inactive time 5 hours | Makes 12 Manchurian balls

INGREDIENTS

Manchurian balls
1 cup (65 g) green cabbage, very thinly chopped
½ cup (70 g) carrot, finely grated
¼ cup (35 g) red bell pepper, very finely chopped
¼ cup (25 g) spring onion, very finely chopped
2 tbsp coconut aminos
1 tbsp ginger, grated
1 garlic clove, minced
1 green rawit pepper, very finely chopped
¼ cup (25 g) blond flax meal
1 tbsp psyllium husk powder

Manchurian sauce
½ portion all-purpose tomato sauce (page 154)
1 green rawit pepper, chopped
1 green onion stalk, chopped
1 tsp ginger, grated
1 garlic clove, minced

Topping
spring onion to taste

METHOD

Gently knead the green cabbage, carrot, red bell pepper, and spring onion in a big bowl until well combined.

Carefully squeeze out the liquid of the vegetable mixture.

Add coconut aminos, ginger, garlic, and pepper to the mixture and combine well.

Add flax meal and psyllium husk powder to the mixture and gently knead them into a dough.

Divide the dough into 12 equal parts and create balls.

Place the Manchurian balls on a dehydrator tray and dehydrate for five hours at 115 °F/46 °C.

In the meantime, make the Manchurian sauce.

Blend the ingredients in a high-speed blender until smooth.

Pour the sauce into a bowl and set it aside.

Place the sauce into the dehydrator when the balls have four more hours to go.

Pour the sauce into a clean bowl, add the Manchurian balls, and top with spring onion.

RAW FOOD FEAST IDEA
Serve the Manchurian balls and sauce with kelp noodles, cauliflower rice, or coodles (cucumber noodles).

BEET BURGER

Enjoy these scrumptious beet burgers together with your favorites. Serve on a portobello bun with lettuce, tomato, cucumber, pickled red onions (page 144), and sweet barbecue sauce (page 116).

Active time 30 minutes | Inactive time 5-7 hours | Makes 4 patties

INGREDIENTS

1½ cups (190 g) beet, chopped
1 cup (140 g) carrot, chopped
½ cup (70 g) red bell pepper, chopped
2 dried figs
½ cup (20 g) parsley, stems and leaves, tightly packed
1 tbsp psyllium husk powder
1 tbsp blond flax meal
1 garlic clove, minced
1 tsp onion powder
1 tsp mustard powder

METHOD

Add the ingredients to a food processor and mix them until well combined.

Divide the mixture into four equal parts, create burgers to your liking, and place them onto a non-stick dehydrator sheet.

Dehydrate the burgers at 145 °F/63 °C for two hours.

Flip the burgers onto another dehydrator tray and carefully remove the non-stick sheet.

Dehydrate the burgers for another 3-5 hours at 115 °F/46 °C.

The beet burgers should be dry on the outside and slightly soft on the inside.

RAW FOOD FEAST TIP
Prepare the portobello bun with the marvelous mushroom marinade (page 153) and top with sesame seeds for extra deliciousness.

ITALIAN MUSHROOM BALLS

Serve Italian mushroom balls at a party fresh out of the dehydrator or chilled. Either way, they taste great. Or spiralize some cucumbers and top with these delicious balls and sauce to enjoy pasta.

Active time 30 minutes | Inactive time 9-11 hours | Makes 20 balls

INGREDIENTS

1 cup (65 g) brown cremini mushrooms, chopped
½ cup (60 g) sunflower seeds, soaked 4 hours
8.5 oz/240 g zucchini, chopped
½ cup (40 g) sundried tomatoes, soaked 4 hours
3 tbsp coconut aminos
1 tbsp dried parsley
2 garlic cloves, minced
1 tsp onion powder
2 tbsp psyllium husk powder

Italian tomato sauce
½ portion all-purpose tomato sauce, page 154
1 tbsp dried parsley

Topping
parsley leaves to taste

METHOD

Add the ingredients, except for the psyllium husk powder, to a food processor and mix them until well combined.

Add the psyllium husk powder to the food processor and blend it into a dough.

Divide the dough into 20 equal parts and create balls.

Place the Italian mushroom balls on a dehydrator tray and dehydrate for five hours at 115 °F/46 °C.

In the meantime, make the Italian tomato sauce.

Blend the ingredients in a high-speed blender until smooth.

Pour the sauce into a bowl and set it aside.

Place the sauce in the dehydrator when the balls have four more hours to go.

Pour the sauce into a clean bowl, add the Italian mushroom balls, and top with parsley leaves.

CROWD PLEASERS

whatever a party heart desires

COCONUT TURMERIC OMELET

Coconut turmeric omelets are a breeze to make and incredibly tasty. You can fill the omelet with leafy greens, non-sweet fruit, and veggies of choice. I used thawed frozen spinach (it creates that wilted look), marvelous mushrooms (page 153), cherry tomatoes, cilantro, and spring onion.

Active time 20-30 minutes | Inactive time 6-8 hours | Makes 2 omelets

INGREDIENTS

2½ cups (250 g) young coconut meat
¼ cup (25 g) blond flax meal
1 tbsp psyllium husk powder
2 tbsp sea moss gel
1 tsp kala namak
1 tsp turmeric powder
¾ cup (180 ml) sunny soak water

METHOD

Add the omelet ingredients to a food processor and mix them into a smooth batter.

Divide the batter into two equal parts and spread evenly onto two non-stick dehydrator sheets, about ¼"/0,5 cm thick.

Dehydrate the omelets for 6-8 hours at 115 °F/46 °C.

Flip the omelets halfway onto other dehydrator trays and carefully remove the non-stick sheets.

The omelets should be pretty dry and pliable.

RAW FOOD FEAST TIP
Lightly wet your hands to form the omelets with ease.

PASTA VERDE

If you want to add more nutrients to your day, this earthy pasta verde is your go-to. The herbs are packed with healing properties, young coconut meat is full of fiber, and hulled hemp seeds are a great source of omega-3 fatty acids and contain all nine essential amino acids, to name a few.

Active time 15 minutes | Makes 1 pasta

INGREDIENTS

2 large zucchini, spiralized

Paste verde sauce
5 oz/150 g cucumber, chopped
½ cup (50 g) young coconut meat
2 tbsp lime juice
1 tbsp coconut vinegar
1 cup (40 g) cilantro, stems and leaves, tightly packed
1 cup (40 g) basil, stems and leaves, tightly packed
½ cup (20 g) Thai basil, stems and leaves, tightly packed
3 tbsp hulled hemp seeds
1 garlic clove, minced

METHOD

Blend the pasta verde sauce ingredients in a high-speed blender until smooth.

Add the zoodles and sauce to a large bowl and combine well.

PINEAPPLE COCONUT CURRY

This healthy pineapple coconut curry is over the moon delicious and perfect in every season of the year. It's great after a warm day spent on the beach or after a long walk in the forest on a cold day. Coconut water contains electrolytes, such as potassium, magnesium, and calcium. Electrolytes are involved in the functioning of the nervous system and muscles. It's one of the reasons why it's good to drink pure coconut water during or after exercising.

Active time 30 minutes | Makes 1-2 curries

INGREDIENTS

Pineapple coconut curry sauce
1 cup (100 g) young coconut meat
1 cup (235 ml) pineapple juice
4 Medjool dates, pitted
1 tsp curry powder
1 tsp ginger, grated
1 garlic clove, minced
½ cup (120 ml) coconut water

Noodles
1 cucumber, spiralized
2 carrots, spiralized

Other ingredients
1 red bell pepper, thinly sliced
1 orange bell pepper, thinly sliced
1 cup (160 g) pineapple, finely chopped

Topping
bean sprouts to taste
spring onion to taste
cilantro leaves to taste
nigella seeds to taste

METHOD

Blend the pineapple coconut curry sauce ingredients in a high-speed blender until smooth.

In the meantime, prepare the noodles and other ingredients, add to a large bowl, and mix well.

Pour the pineapple coconut curry sauce into a bowl and add the noodle mixture.

Top the pineapple coconut curry with bean sprouts, spring onion, cilantro leaves, and nigella seeds.

WILD RICE BLOOMING BOWL

Wild rice, a type of grass, is an incredible source of nutrients. It's full of antioxidants, micronutrients, such as magnesium, folate (a B vitamin), and zinc, but also packed with fiber.
The great thing about wild rice is that you can eat it raw by soaking it in water. This process is named blooming since wild rice does not sprout. Blooming softens and swells the rice as if it's cooked.

Active time 30-35 minutes | Inactive time 24 hours | Makes 2 portions

INGREDIENTS

Blooming bowl ingredients
½ cup (80 g) wild rice, rinsed and bloomed
6 oz/180 g red cabbage, thinly sliced
1 medium carrot, julienne cut
½ cup (100 g) fresh wakame
½ mango, finely chopped
1 avocado, thinly sliced

Ginger tahini vinaigrette
¼ cup (60 ml) tahini
¼ cup (60 ml) coconut vinegar
2 tbsp date paste
1 tbsp coconut aminos
1 tbsp ginger, grated
1 tsp onion powder
1 tsp garlic powder

Topping
bean sprouts to taste
spring onion to taste
sesame seeds to taste
chili flakes to taste
dulse granules to taste

METHOD

Rinse the wild rice thoroughly, add to a large mason jar, and fill with water to the brim.

Place the jar in the dehydrator for 24 hours at 115°F/46 °C. Do not use a lid.

Prepare the other blooming bowl ingredients and ginger tahini vinaigrette 30 minutes before the blooming process is ready.

Blend the ingredients of the ginger tahini vinaigrette in a high-speed blender until smooth.

Rinse the bloomed wild rice and pet dry.

Add two tablespoons of the ginger tahini vinaigrette to the bloomed wild rice and mix well.

If you want to plate like this, use a cooking ring (Ø 4"/10 cm). First, add the bloomed wild rice, then carrot, red cabbage, wakame, mango, and finish with avocado. Gently remove the cooking ring.

Sprinkle the tahini vinaigrette onto the wild blooming bowl and top it along with the bean sprouts, spring onion, sesame seeds, chili flakes, and dulse granules.

RAW FOOD FEAST TIP
You can get wild rice at most organic food stores or online.

ASIAN-STYLE PANCAKES

If I doubted I was Dutch, I would think I was at least half Asian. I simply love the Asian kitchen.
The incredible taste of its flavorful food makes my heart happy. I hope that once you set your teeth into
these Asian-style pancakes, your heart and taste buds will jump for joy too.
It's a perfect crowd pleaser, or enjoy it alone with the door shut. Completely understandable.

Active time 15-20 minutes | Inactive time 6-8 hours | Makes 10 pancakes

INGREDIENTS

Pancake batter
2½ cups (250 g) young coconut meat
¼ cup (25 g) blond flax meal
1½ cups (355 ml) sunny soak water
2 tbsp sea moss gel
½ tbsp psyllium husk powder
½ tsp kala namak

Veggie mix
1 medium carrot, match sticks or
julienne cut
1 red bell pepper, thinly sliced
1 bunch of spring onion, coarsely
chopped
1 green rawit pepper, thinly sliced

Dipping sauce
1 tbsp coconut aminos
1 tbsp coconut vinegar or apple
cider vinegar
1 tbsp water
1 tsp date paste
1/2 tsp sesame seeds
1/2 tsp chili flakes (optional)

METHOD

Add the pancake batter ingredients to a food processor and mix
them into a smooth batter.

In the meantime, prepare the veggie mix and add to a large bowl.

Pour the pancake batter on top of the veggie mix and combine well.

Scoop ⅓ cup of the mixture onto a non-stick dehydrator sheet
and spread it evenly into a 4"/10 cm shaped pancake.

Dehydrate the pancakes at 145 °F/63 °C for two hours.

Flip the pancakes onto other dehydrator trays and carefully remove
the non-stick sheets.

Dehydrate the pancakes for another 4-6 hours at 115 °F/46 °C.
The pancakes should be slightly moist.

Add the dipping sauce ingredients to a small bowl and whisk until
combined.

Gather some loved ones and dip your Asian-style pancakes in the
sauce. Enjoy!

BELL PEPPER PIZZA

Everyone loves pizza, so if you happen to throw a party make a bunch of pizzas and you'll have a happy crowd. You can use any topping you like.

Active time 30 minutes | Inactive time 8 hours | Makes 2 pizzas

INGREDIENTS

Pizza crust ingredients
7 oz/ 200 g red bell pepper, chopped
10.5 oz/300 g Roma tomatoes, chopped
2 tbsp psyllium husk powder
2 garlic cloves, minced
½ cup (120 ml) water

Topping
½ portion all-purpose tomato sauce, page 154
1 tbsp dried parsley
2 cups (125 g) mushrooms, sliced
12 mini Roma tomatoes, sliced
½ cup (70 g) pineapple, finely chopped
arugula to taste
parsley to taste

METHOD

Add the pizza crust ingredients to a food processor and mix them into a smooth dough.

In the meantime, prepare the all-purpose tomato sauce.

Divide the dough into two equal parts and spread evenly onto two non-stick dehydrator sheets, about ¼"/0,5 cm thick.

Dehydrate the pizza crusts for two hours at 145 °F/63 °C.

Flip the pizza crusts onto other dehydrator trays and carefully remove the non-stick sheets.

Dehydrate the pizza crusts for another six hours at 115 °F/46 °C.

Remove the pizzas after four hours from the dehydrator and cut them into slices. A scissor works great to create slices.

First, add the all-purpose tomato sauce and dried parsley onto the pizza crusts. Next, add the other toppings, except for the arugula and parsley, and continue the dehydration process.

Top the bell pepper pizza with arugula and parsley.

RAW FOOD FEAST TIP
Use marvelous mushrooms, page 153, as topping for extra flavor. You don't need to dehydrate the mushrooms first as the recipe calls for; simply add them onto the pizza with the other toppings.

BALSAMIC ONION SPREAD

This spread is downright delicious and o so versatile. I love to use this spread on wraps especially. It gives a full and rich taste without overpowering. Enjoy the deliciousness!

Active time 10 minutes | Inactive time 10 hours | Makes about 1 cup (250 ml)

INGREDIENTS

Spread
1 cup (120 g) cashew nuts, soaked 8 hours
1 shallot, finely chopped
½ cup (120 ml) water

Marinade
2 tbsp balsamic vinegar
1 tbsp date paste
1 small garlic clove, minced
1 tsp onion powder

METHOD

Add the balsamic marinade ingredients to a small bowl and whisk until combined.

Pour the balsamic marinade on top of the shallot and mix well.

Marinate the shallot overnight in the fridge.

Place the shallot onto a non-stick dehydrator sheet. Keep the marinade for later.

Dehydrate the shallot at 105 °F/41 °C for 2 hours.

Blend the ingredients, including the remains of the marinade, in a high-speed blender until smooth.

Store the balsamic onion spread in a mason jar in the fridge.

RAW FOOD FEAST TIP
Soak the cashew nuts overnight as the shallot marinates to save time.

SWEET BARBECUE SAUCE

This healthy and sweet barbecue sauce makes any burger top-notch. Let's go and make some.

Active time 5 minutes | Inactive time 4 hours | Makes about 1 cup (250 ml)

INGREDIENTS

4 roma tomatoes, chopped
¼ cup (20 g) sundried tomatoes,
soaked 4 hours
6 Medjool dates, pitted
2 tbsp lime juice
1 tbsp tahini
1 garlic clove, minced
1 tsp Italian herbs
1 tsp sweet paprika powder
1 tsp onion powder
½ tsp chili flakes
2 tbsp water

METHOD

Blend the ingredients in a high-speed blender until smooth.

Store the sweet barbecue sauce in a mason jar in the fridge.

DANCE AND DIP
THE NIGHT AWAY

let's boogie and dip

CARDAMOM FIG BROWNIES

Chewy, sweet, and scrumptious, exactly how brownies are supposed to be.

Active time 20 minutes | Inactive time 10 hours | Makes 6 brownies

INGREDIENTS

½ cup (50 g) pecan nuts, soaked
4 hours
½ cup (50 g) walnuts, soaked 4 hours
10 Medjool dates, pitted
4 dried figs
¼ cup (50 g) carob powder
½ tbsp cardamom powder

Topping
pecan nuts and/or walnuts to taste,
finely chopped

METHOD

Add the cardamom fig brownies ingredients to a food processor and mix until it forms a ball.

Pour the dough on a flat surface, such as a cutting board, and form it into a rectangle.

Place the cutting board with the brownie in the fridge for 6 hours.

Cut the brownie into six equal pieces.

Top the cardamom fig brownies with the nuts.

Store the cardamom fig brownies in the fridge.

SWEET
CELEBRATIONS

the perfect afterparty

ARTICHOKE SPINACH DIP

Serve this creamy, healthy artichoke spinach dip with Indian tortilla chips (page 62) and your favorite non-sweet fruits, like cucumber, bell pepper, and tomato. Enjoy!

Active time 5-10 minutes | Inactive time 8 hours | Makes about 1 cup (250 ml)

INGREDIENTS

6 artichoke hearts, chopped
3.5 oz/100 g spinach, thawed from frozen
½ cup (70 g) macadamia nuts, soaked 4 hours
¼ cup (15 g) nutritional yeast
1 garlic clove, minced
2 tbsp sunny soak water

Topping
chili flakes to taste

METHOD

Blend the artichoke spinach dip ingredients in a high-speed blender until smooth.

Pour the artichoke spinach dip into a bowl and top with chili flakes.

Store the artichoke spinach dip in an airtight container in the fridge.

FRESH TZATZIKI

This fresh tzatziki, with a twist, is not just tasty but also healthy and nutritious. Hemp seeds contain all essential amino acids. Fresh herbs have all sorts of incredible properties too. For example, parsley contains lots of betacarotene, mint is full of antioxidants, and dill stimulates digestion.

Active time 5-10 minutes | Makes about 1 cup (250 ml)

INGREDIENTS

½ cucumber, linseeds removed, chopped
¼ cup (30 g) hulled hemp seeds
2 tbsp lime juice
1 tbsp tahini
1 tbsp green salt
1 garlic clove, minced
1 tbsp parsley leaves, finely chopped
1 tbsp mint leaves, finely chopped
1 tbsp dill leaves, finely chopped

METHOD

Add the ingredients, except for the fresh herbs, to a blender and blend until smooth.

Add the herbs and combine well.

Store the fresh tzatziki in an air-tight container in the fridge.

Dip away with your veggies of choice.

SUNDRIED TOMATO TAPENADE

This fresh sundried tomato tapenade is perfect to serve on a slice of buckwheat bread (page 70) or on top of the sprouted almond bagels (page 76).

Active time 10-15 minutes | Inactive time 8 hours | Makes about 1 cup (300 ml)

INGREDIENTS

Tapenade
1 red bell pepper, finely chopped
1 cup (80 g) sundried tomatoes, soaked 8 hours, finely chopped
1 cup (40 g) basil leaves, tightly packed, finely chopped
3 spring onion sprigs, finely chopped
1 garlic clove, minced

Marinade
¼ cup (60 ml) lime juice
2 tbsp date paste
2 tbsp pomegranate syrup
½ tsp chili flakes

METHOD

Prepare the tapenade ingredients and add them to a large bowl.

Add the marinade ingredients to a small bowl and whisk until combined.

Pour the marinade on top of the tapenade ingredients and mix well.

Store the sundried tomato tapenade in a mason jar in the fridge.

DILL CAPER CASHEW CREAM

I adore both dill and capers, so this is one of my favorite spreads. Use dill caper cashew cream on za'atar flatbread (page 75), a wrap, or add to a salad. Or scoop it straight into your mouth. It's sooo good!

Active time 5-10 minutes | Inactive time 16-20 hours | Makes about 1 cup (250 ml)

INGREDIENTS

1 cup (120 g) cashew nuts, soaked 8 hours
½ cup (120 ml) water
1½ tsp soil-based probiotic powder
½ cup (60 g) capers, finely chopped
½ cup (15 g) dill leaves, finely chopped

METHOD

Blend the cashew nuts, water, and probiotic powder in a high-speed blender until smooth.

Pour the cashew cream into a mason jar, put a piece of parchment paper on top, and gently press it onto the cashew cream.
Do not close with a lid. The cashew cream should air during this process.

Store the cashew cream in a warm spot for 8-12 hours. When the cashew cream smells slightly sour and is pretty thick, it's ready.

Add capers and dill leaves to the cashew cream and combine well.

Store the dill caper cashew cream in a mason jar in the fridge.

RAW FOOD FEAST TIP
Pop the mason jar on top of your dehydrator while it's on.
It's the perfect warmth to create a beautiful cashew cream.

SPROUTED LENTIL HUMMUS

Hummus is always a good idea. It is tasty, healthy, and satiating. You can use it as a spread on crackers (page 72 and 81), on a slice of buckwheat bread (page 70), or create a wild rice blooming bowl (see page 109 how to bloom wild rice) topped with sprouted lentil hummus.

Active time 5-10 minutes | Inactive time 5-7 days | Makes about 2 cups (500 ml)

INGREDIENTS

¼ cup (50 g) green lentils, soaked and sprouted*
¼ cup (30 g) sunflower seeds, soaked
¼ cup (60 ml) tahini
¼ cup (60 ml) lime juice
2 garlic cloves, minced
1 tbsp green salt
½ tsp cumin powder
½ tsp turmeric powder
½ tsp paprika powder
2-4 tbsp water, optionally

METHOD

Blend the sprouted lentil hummus ingredients, except for the water, in a high-speed blender until smooth. Add only water if needed. Start with two tablespoons when the hummus is too dry. Whether you need water depends on if you use thick or runny tahini.

Store the sprouted lentil hummus in an air-tight container in the fridge.

RAW FOOD FEAST FACT
*A ¼ cup green lentils yields about 2 cups of sprouted green lentils. You need 2 cups of sprouted lentils to create this recipe. The same goes for the sprouted lentil burgers on page 86 and falafel on page 90.

BALSAMIC ONION SPREAD

This spread is downright delicious and o so versatile. I love to use this spread on wraps especially.
It gives a full and rich taste without overpowering. Enjoy the deliciousness!

Active time 10 minutes | Inactive time 10 hours | Makes about 1 cup (250 ml)

INGREDIENTS

Spread
1 cup (120 g) cashew nuts, soaked
8 hours
1 shallot, finely chopped
½ cup (120 ml) water

Marinade
2 tbsp balsamic vinegar
1 tbsp date paste
1 small garlic clove, minced
1 tsp onion powder

METHOD

Add the balsamic marinade ingredients to a small bowl and whisk until combined.

Pour the balsamic marinade on top of the shallot and mix well.

Marinate the shallot overnight in the fridge.

Place the shallot onto a non-stick dehydrator sheet. Keep the marinade for later.

Dehydrate the shallot at 105 °F/41 °C for 2 hours.

Blend the ingredients, including the remains of the marinade, in a high-speed blender until smooth.

Store the balsamic onion spread in a mason jar in the fridge.

RAW FOOD FEAST TIP

Soak the cashew nuts overnight as the shallot marinates to save time.

RASPBERRY CHOCOLATE MOUSSE

This raspberry chocolate mousse is such a joy. It's tasty and healthy.
A perfect mousse to enjoy with your family or a bunch of friends.

Active time 5-10 minutes | Inactive time 16 hours | Makes 4 portions

INGREDIENTS

0,5 oz/15 g dehydrated sea moss,
soaked 12 hours
1 cup (120 g) cashew nuts, soaked
8 hours
1½ cups (230 g) raspberries, frozen
2 tbsp carob powder
3-4 tbsp date paste
1 cup (235 ml) sea moss soak water

Topping
raspberries to taste

METHOD

Blend the raspberry chocolate mousse ingredients in a high-speed blender until smooth.

Divide the mousse over four glasses and let it sit in the fridge for 4 hours.

Top the raspberry chocolate mousse with raspberries.

APPLE CRUMBLE MINI PIES

Apple crumble pie is always a good idea. It's loved by many and devoured in minutes.
If you want to make a big apple crumble pie instead of mini's, use a 10"/26 cm pie pan.

Active time 45 minutes | Inactive time 9 hours | Makes 8 4"/10 cm mini pies

INGREDIENTS

8 Granny Smith apples, thinly sliced
¼ cup (60 ml) lime juice
1 tbsp cardamom powder
¼ cup (60 ml) date paste

Apple pie crust and crumble
2 cups (240 g) almonds, soaked
8 hours
1 cup (100 g) walnuts, soaked
8 hours
½ cup (80 g) dried cranberries
½ cup (80 g) raisins
2 tbsp date paste

METHOD

Add the apple slices and the lime juice to a large bowl and combine well.

Coat the apple slices evenly with cardamom powder.

Spread the apple slices evenly onto three or four dehydrator trays and dehydrate them for 2 hours at 105 °F/41 °C.

In the meantime, prepare the apple pie crust and crumble ingredients with a food processor into a slightly chunky mixture.

Keep 2 cups (280 g) apple pie crumble aside and use the rest to make the crust.

Store the crust and crumble mixture in the fridge until the apple slices are ready.

Add the apple slices and date paste to a large bowl and combine well.

Divide the apple pie crust mixture into eight equal parts.

Create the apple crumble mini pies on serving plates.

Place a cooking ring (Ø 4"/10 cm) on a plate, add the apple pie crust mixture evenly, and press the crust into the mold.

Divide the apple slices into eight equal parts, add them evenly onto the apple pie crust, and press the apple slices lightly into the crust.

Top the pie with the apple pie crumble and gently press the crumble onto the apple slices.

Carefully remove the cooking rings from the apple crumble mini pie.

BANANA ROLLS

Banana rolls are a breeze to make and fun to bring along to a party or picnic. Whenever using bananas, make sure the peel has brown spots. It's a sign of a ripe banana.

Active time 15 minutes | Inactive time 14-16 hours | Makes 12 rolls

INGREDIENTS

12 large bananas, sliced

Medjool spread
5 Medjool dates, pitted
¼ cup (40 g) raisins
1 tbsp carob powder
1-2 tbsp water, optional

Vanilla coconut drizzle
1 cup (100 g) young coconut meat
¼ cup (60 ml) coconut water
seeds of 1 vanilla bean

Topping
walnuts to taste, finely chopped

METHOD

Cut each banana into three slices.

Place the banana slices on dehydrator trays and dehydrate for 7-9 hours at 105 °F/41 °C. The banana slices should be soft and pliable.

In the meantime, prepare the Medjool spread and vanilla coconut drizzle.

Blend the Medjool spread ingredients in a high-speed blender until smooth. If the Medjool spread is dry, add some water, starting with one tablespoon first, and mix well.

Blend the vanilla coconut drizzle ingredients in a high-speed blender until smooth.

Store the Medjool spead and vanilla coconut drizzle in the fridge until use.

Add a thin layer of the Medjool spread on a banana slice and roll it. Repeat this process. However, this time fold the banana slice around the other banana slice. Each roll is one banana, so three slices per banana roll.

Place the banana rolls on a dehydrator tray and dehydrate for another 7 hours at 105 °F/41 °C.

Top the banana rolls with vanilla coconut drizzle and walnuts.

RAW FOOD FEAST TIP
Feel free to add other ingredients to the Medjool spread, such as cardamom or cinnamon powder.

MANGO CHEESECAKE BARS

The rich taste of the carob nut crust and the fresh soft taste of mango and lime combined are a match made in paradise. Any get-together becomes a hit when serving mango cheesecake bars.

Active time 30 minutes | Inactive time 6 hours | Makes 24 bars

INGREDIENTS

Carob nut crust
½ cup of each: almonds (60 g),
cashew nuts (60 g), walnuts (50 g),
soaked 8 hours
¼ cup + 2 tbsp (60 g) carob powder
5 Medjool dates, pitted
¼ cup (60 ml) date paste

Mango filling
2 cups (240 g) cashew nuts, soaked
8 hours
1 cup (100 g) young coconut meat
½ cup (120 ml) coconut water
3 cups (420 g) mango, chopped
¼ cup (60 ml) lime juice
¼ cup (60 ml) date paste
¼ cup (45 g) psyllium husk powder
3 tbsp sunflower lechitin

Raspberry drizzle
1 cup (140 g) raspberries
1 tbsp date paste
1 tbsp lime juice

METHOD

Add the carob nut crust ingredients to a food processor and mix them into a slightly chunky mixture.

Distribute the crust evenly to a pan and lightly press the crust.

Blend the mango filling ingredients in a high-speed blender until smooth.

Pour the mango filling evenly on top of the crust.

Place the mango cheesecake in the freezer for six hours.

In the meantime, make the raspberry drizzle and store it in the fridge until use.

Top the mango cheesecake with the raspberry drizzle and cut it into 24 bars.

Serve the mango cheese cake bars chilled.

RAW FOOD FEAST FACT
Sunflower lecithin is an emulsifier that helps to bind the ingredients. The great thing about sunflower lecithin is that it's non-GMO, raw, and naturally extracted (without chemical use) from sunflower seeds. Sunflower lecithin is available in most organic food stores or online.

FESTIVE FLAVORS

add-ons for some extra soul

PICKLED RED ONIONS

Pickled red onions are about to become your best friend and household staple.
This fresh, sour delight brightens up any dish. Literally.

Active time 5-10 minutes | Inactive time 8 hours | Makes 2 cups (280 g) pickled red onions

INGREDIENTS

3 red onions, thinly sliced
coconut vinegar

METHOD

Use a mandoline or food processor to create thin onion rings and place them in a mason jar.

Pour coconut vinegar on top of the onions until they are covered.

Marinate the onions overnight in the fridge.

The pickled red onions can be kept in the fridge for 2-3 weeks, as long as they are stored covered with vinegar and a lid.

GARLIC CROUTONS

Add garlic croutons to salads or soups for that extra crunch and flavor.
Feel free to add other dried herbs, such as oregano, thyme, or basil.

Active time 15-20 minutes | Inactive time 2-3 days | Makes about 100 croutons

INGREDIENTS

¼ cup (45 g) buckwheat kernels,
soaked and sprouted
½ cup (75 g) blond flax seeds
¼ cup (60 ml) sunny soak water to
soak flax seeds
2 tbsp blond flax meal
1 tbsp psyllium husk powder
1 tsp sea moss gel
2 garlic cloves, minced
2 tbsp dried parsley
1 tsp onion powder
1 tsp garlic powder
2 tbsp sunny soak water

Topping
1 tbsp dried parsley

METHOD

Blend the garlic croutons ingredients in a food processor into a
dough until it forms a ball.

Spread the dough evenly onto a non-stick dehydrator sheet,
about ½"/1 cm thick, and score into small pieces.

Flip the croutons onto another dehydrator sheet and carefully
remove the non-stick sheet.

Gently separate the croutons.

Top the croutons with dried parsley.

Dehydrate the croutons first at 145 °F/63 °C for two hours and
then for another 1-3 hours at 115 °F/46 °C.

The garlic croutons should have a crunch.

Store the garlic croutons in an airtight container.

MARINATED CARROTS

Marinated carrots are simply amazing. You can add them to bagels (page 76), salads, wraps,
or cucumber roll-ups (page 54), for example.
I like marinated carrots with a crunch, but here are some tips on how to soften carrots without cooking.
Place the carrot strips in a container, pour hot water over the carrot strips, and let them sit for 30 minutes.
Pat them dry and add the marinade. Or freeze the carrots overnight and let them thaw.
Pat the carrot strips dry and add the marinade. Easy like that.

Active time 10-15 minutes | Inactive time 8 hours | Makes 4 portions

INGREDIENTS

35 oz/1 kg carrots, strips

Marinade
3 tbsp coconut aminos
1 tbsp date paste
½ tbsp liquid smoke
1 tsp dulse granules

METHOD

Use a vegetable peeler or food processor to create thin carrot strips and place them in a container.

Add the marinade ingredients to a small bowl and whisk until combined.

Pour the marinade on top of the carrot strips and massage the strips with your hands until the marinade is fully combined.

Marinate the carrots strips overnight in the fridge.

GREEN SALT

Regular table salt is never a good idea. Table salt is stripped of most minerals, unlike other salts, such as Himalaya salt or Celtic sea salt. However, that doesn't mean it's all that great to use salt.
Your cells need to maintain a certain ratio of sodium to potassium.
Adding salt continuously to your food will negatively affect those ratios. Fruit, leafy greens, veg, nuts, and seeds will provide the sodium (and potassium) you need, including healthy ratios.
Another side effect of salt is that it fools your taste buds. It stimulates your taste buds so that you won't notice in time that your body is satiated. Overeating is a result, and often weight gain too.
It's best to minimize the use of Himalaya or Celtic sea salt or omit it entirely. However, never use table salt.
I like to make a salt substitute, which I label green salt, by dehydrating Salicornia cress.
Salicornia is a healthy, high-fiber salt substitute. A beautiful gift from the sea.

Active time 5 minutes | Inactive time 24-28 hours | Makes about ½ cup (30 g) green salt

INGREDIENTS

10.5 oz/300 g Salicornia cress

METHOD

Place the Salicornia cress evenly onto dehydrator trays.

Dehydrate the Salicornia cress at 105 °F/41 °C for 24-28 hours. The Salicornia cress should be completely dry.

Grind the Salicornia cress in a herb grinder.

Store the green salt in an airtight container.

RAW FOOD FEAST TIP
You can buy ready-made Salicornia salt at your organic food store. It is also known as glasswort or samphire salt. Otherwise, you can order it online.

MARVELOUS MUSHROOMS

Marvelous mushrooms are just that: marvelous. They add body to a delicious salad, that umami experience to a raw food burger, and make a wrap taste even better.

Active time 5 minutes | Inactive time 2 hours | Makes about 4 portions

INGREDIENTS

4 cups (250 g) brown cremini mushrooms, sliced

Marinade
3 tbsp coconut aminos
1 tbsp date paste
½ tsp sweet paprika powder
¼ tsp ground black pepper

METHOD

Add the ingredients to a big bowl and gently massage the mushrooms with the marinade until well combined.

Spread the mushrooms evenly onto a non-stick dehydrator sheet and dehydrate at 105 °F/41 °C for two hours.

Store the marvelous mushrooms in an air-tight container in the fridge.

RAW FOOD FEAST TIP
You can also use shiitake, portobellos, or oyster mushrooms.

ALL-PURPOSE TOMATO SAUCE

Use this all-purpose tomato sauce just as it is or add other delicious ingredients as I did with the Manchurian sauce (page 94). Combine this sauce with coodles (cucumber noodles) to create a marinara dish. Stir it through some veggies and marinate in the dehydrator for 1-2 hours. It is also perfect as a pizza base sauce (page 112). The options are endless.

Active time 5-10 minutes | Inactive time 10 hours | Makes about 3 cups (750 ml) sauce

INGREDIENTS

14 oz/400 g Roma tomatoes, chopped
1 red bell pepper, chopped
¼ cup (20 g) sundried tomatoes, soaked 8 hours
5 Medjool dates, pitted
1 tbsp coconut vinegar
1 small garlic clove, minced
1 tsp dried oregano
½ tsp chili flakes

METHOD

Blend the ingredients in a high-speed blender into a chunky or smooth consistency.

Pour the sauce into a bowl and dehydrate at 145 °F/63 °C for two hours.

Store the all-purpose tomato sauce in a mason jar in an airtight container in the fridge.

RAW FOOD FEAST FACT
The dehydration process makes the flavors more intense, warms, and creates a gorgeous thick tomato sauce.

DATE PASTE

Date paste is so versatile. You can use it in all sorts of recipes to add some sweetness. It also gives extra body to a dressing, dip, or sauce. Use soft Medjool dates to create the paste. If the dates are dry, soak them first in water for 30 minutes.

Active time 5-10 minutes | Makes about 1 cup (250 ml)

INGREDIENTS

20 Medjool dates, pitted
1 cup (235 ml) water

METHOD

Blend the date paste ingredients in a high-speed blender until smooth.

Store the date paste in an airtight container in the fridge.

Index

Index

Index

Index

Index

Index

Index

Colophon

Text and recipes

Mirjam Henzen

Styling and photography

Mirjam Henzen

Cover design

Mirjam Henzen

ISBN 9789083092270

NUR 444

© 2023 Mirjam Henzen

© 2023 Publishing House Eden

www.rawfoodfeast.com

Raw Food Feast Playlist
https://spoti.fi/3ZMDHki

Do you love mouthwatering foods, inspiring information, and helpful tips?
Come and follow Raw Food Feast on Instagram @rawfoodfeast.

Made in the USA
Las Vegas, NV
19 April 2023

70820648R00100